LET NOT YOUR

Heart

BE T

KEITH *&* JAKE PROVANCE

Let Not Your Heart Be Troubled
ISBN: 978-1-939570-80-2
Copyright © 2017 by Word and Spirit Publishing

Published by Word and Spirit Publishing
P.O. Box 701403
Tulsa, Oklahoma 74170
wordandspiritpublishing.com

CONTENTS

Introduction.. v

Let Not Your Heart Be Troubled.................... 1

Happiness Is a Choice................................... 7

Help.. 13

Knocked Down, but Not Out 19

Loss.. 25

Don't Quit 31

Thankfulness 37

Trapped 43

Weariness 49

Discouragement 55

The Past.. 61

It's a Choice 67

About the Authors

Keith Provance, involved in Christian publishing for more than 30 years, is the founder and president of Word and Spirit Publishing, a company dedicated to the publishing and world-wide distribution of scriptural, life-changing books. He also works as a publishing consultant to national and international ministries. Keith continues to write with his wife and with his son Jake. He and his wife, Megan, have authored a number of best-selling books with total sales of over 2 million copies. They reside in Tulsa, Oklahoma and are the parents of three sons, Ryan, Garrett. and Jake.

You may contact Keith at
Keith@WordAndSpiritPublishing.com

Jake Provance is an avid reader and an aspiring young writer, who has written five books and has plans to write several more. Jake's first book, Keep Calm & Trust God, has sold more than 500,000 copies. Jake is a graduate of Domata Bible School in Tulsa, OK, and has a call on his life to work in pastoral care ministry, with a particular passion to minister to young adults. Jake and his wife, Leah, live in Tulsa, OK.

Check out Jake's blog at Life-Speak.com

You may contact Jake at
Jake@WordAndSpiritPublishing.com

INTRODUCTION

In this world, our lives are under a constant assault—mentally, emotionally, and physically. Every day there are reports of shootings, terror attacks, and unfathomable crimes committed against innocent people. Social media intensifies conflict and division, while piling on the pressure to conform to the status quo in order to be considered an upstanding citizen, parent, spouse, employee, or friend. Add to all of this the exceptionally busy lifestyle that is the hallmark of our culture, and it is little wonder that so many people battle fear, anxiety, and depression on a daily basis.

We all face the temptation to let the turmoil, heartache, and all the filth of this sinful world work its way into our hearts.

When Jesus said, "Let not your heart be troubled," He knew that we would be faced daily with the opportunity to be troubled, but He also knew that we had the ability to choose to guard our hearts and be happy in the midst of trouble because of our unwavering trust in God to see us through. That's why we are to shield ourselves from doubt, from worry, from anxiety, and from fear.

Worry, though often viewed as a well-intentioned display of concern over the unknown, is actually doubting God's willingness or ability to come through. God doesn't want you to stress out with worrying—it causes harm to your body, and destroys your joy! Don't doubt God's love for you, don't doubt His faithfulness on your behalf.

Instead, let go of your cares, your worries, and your pain. Cast them on the Lord. Let God heal your heart from any past mistakes, or past hurts. Then shield it from the pressures of this life by meditating on His Word instead of the issues at hand. Shield it by keeping your eyes focused on Him, in worship and in prayer, instead of all the crazy things happening in the world. Count on Him to see you through, to be your Friend and your Father.

It is never God's will for us to be plagued with anxiety and fear. It has never been His will for us to be depressed or stressed. It is His will for us to live freely, with abundant evidence of His grace, mercy, and goodness in our lives. Let go of all your troubles and embrace freedom and joy!

"Do not let your hearts be troubled. Trust in God; trust also in me."

—Jesus Christ

LET NOT YOUR HEART
BE TROUBLED

It's simple, really. God loves you very much. And He never wants you to feel worried about your future, about your kids, or about your circumstances. He wants you to trust Him with those things. He never wants you to be depressed or in despair. He wants you to take refuge in Him. He never wanted you to be alone; He traded the life of His most precious Son, and all the suffering He had to endure, just so you could have a relationship with Him every day on this earth . . . stretching into all of eternity. God has given us all good things and desires nothing more than for us to accept His gifts, run into His arms, and be His child. Quit letting your heart be troubled by what you see and hear, and let your heart be comforted by the words of our Father God.

There is no mistake you have made, no sin you have committed, that is more powerful than what Jesus did for you. There is no place that His love can't find you. Depression, despair, and fear have no claim on your life. Worry, anxiety, and stress can't exist in the presence of the peace left for you by our Lord and Savior. God is with you, He is for you, and He will help you through His Word.

There is a freedom, a comfort, a hope, a strength, a healing, a security, and a quiet confidence that is obtained and maintained through the life-giving power of the Word of God. It rewrites the mistakes of your past with the successes of Jesus' past. It places a new identity within you, puts a powerful force to work for you, and bestows blessings upon you. Dare to give in to the life-giving Word of God. Dare to let go of the fear, worry, and anxiety. And finally, dare to let not your heart be troubled.

<u>Prayer</u>

Lord, I ask for Your help with keeping my heart safe. I know it's up to me to protect my heart, but I ask for Your help to discern the good from the bad. Teach me the way I should go. If there are things that would desensitize me to Your voice, or things that are potentially harmful to my heart, I ask that You would tell me so that I may choose You over it. I cast all my cares, all the weights I have carried, and all my confusion on You, Lord. I relinquish my problems and all the mental anguish that comes along with them into Your capable hands. I choose to live freely and lightly in Your loving embrace. Thank You for Your help. Amen.

Scriptures

"Peace I leave with you; My own peace I now give and bequeath to you. Not as the world gives do I give to you. **Do not let your hearts be troubled, neither let them be afraid.** Stop allowing yourselves to be agitated and disturbed; and do not permit yourselves to be fearful and intimidated and cowardly and unsettled."

—John 14:27 AMPC

Guard your heart above all else, for it determines the course of your life.

—Proverbs 4:23 NLT

My child, listen and be wise: keep your heart on the right course.

—Proverbs 23:19 NLT

LET NOT YOUR HEART BE TROUBLED
by Deborah Ann

Let not your heart be troubled,
let not worry start your day
for Jesus came to give you
a new and peaceful way.

Let not concern unsettle you,
let not stress take its toll
for Jesus is here to calm you
and give quietness to your soul.

Let not your mind be burdened,
let not anguish weigh you down
for Jesus you can depend on
His tranquility is all around.

Let not your spirit fail you,
let not despair be what you feel
for Jesus desires your whole heart
to restore ~ so He can heal.

Let not your heart be troubled,
let not it be afraid today
for Jesus will bring you peace
and your anxiety will fade away.

"Everybody in the world is seeking happiness—and there is one sure way to find it. That is by controlling your thoughts. Happiness doesn't depend on outward conditions. It depends on inner conditions."

—DALE CARNEGIE

HAPPINESS IS A CHOICE

The truth is, happiness is a choice independent of your circumstances—not the product of them. When you are robbed of your security through crisis, when the ever-present pain in your body causes you to doubt God's goodness, when the dull grind of life leaves you numb to the joy of being alive, it is up to you and you alone. Either you will choose to let your circumstances dictate your attitude, or you will rise above it all and choose to be happy. It takes courage to dream big when you live small, and it takes strength to find happiness in the midst of pain.

For most people, their happiness—or lack thereof—is dependent upon their circumstances. If things are good, they are happy; if things are not good, then they are not. This will cause them to be up one moment and down the next, happy one day and depressed the next. This emotional rollercoaster lifestyle is no way to live your life! Live like this for any length of time and you'll find yourself stressed out, tired, and weak.

It's not a matter of ignoring difficulties, feigning happiness in the face of adversity, or trying to find a reason why your problem is really a blessing in disguise. Choosing happiness is choosing to base your joy, your security, and your peace on the solid foundation of the Word of God. It's choosing to remember all the benefits and blessings afforded to you as a child of God. It's choosing to trust that God has your back, to smile in the midst of trying times because you have faith in your God! So count your blessings instead of your hurts, begin to fill your words with thanksgiving instead of complaining, and choose to be happy!

Prayer

Lord, Thank You for my life and for my salvation. Thank You for making me Your child. I ask that You draw me near to You. Help me to live in the light of all that You have done, and are doing for me. Remind me to look to You and Your Word instead of my circumstance. Help me to cast my cares on You, and to trust You with them completely. I ask that as I choose to be happy regardless of what is going on in my life, that You will use me as a beacon of hope that will draw people closer to You because they themselves want to find the happiness that can only be found in You. You are my smile, Lord. Thank You. Amen!

Scriptures

Friends, when life gets really difficult, don't jump to the conclusion that God isn't on the job. Instead, be glad that you are in the very thick of what Christ experienced. This is a spiritual refining process, with glory just around the corner.

—1 Peter 4:12-13 MSG

Enjoy the Lord, and he will give what your heart asks.

—Psalm 37:4 CEB

Rejoice in the Lord always delight, gladden yourselves in Him; again I say, Rejoice!

—Philippians 4:4 AMPC

Dear brothers and sisters, when troubles of any kind come your way, consider it an opportunity for great joy. For you know that when your faith is tested, your endurance has a chance to grow. So let it grow, for when your endurance is fully developed, you will be perfect and complete, needing nothing.

—James 1:2-4 NLT

"Happiness is a choice, not a result. Nothing will make you happy until you choose to be happy. No person will make you happy unless you decide to be happy. Your happiness will not come to you. It can only come from you."

—Ralph Marston

For He God Himself has said, I will not in any way fail you nor give you up nor leave you without support. I will not, I will not, I will not in any degree leave you helpless nor forsake nor let [you] down (relax My hold on you)! Assuredly not! So we take comfort and are encouraged and confidently and boldly say, The Lord is my Helper; I will not be seized with alarm I will not fear or dread or be terrified. What can man do to me?

—Hebrews 13:5(b)-6 AMPC

HELP

We all need help. You are not weak because you need help, nor for asking for help. God made us to need Him and each other. Even Jesus fell under the weight of the cross; He needed help to carry out His destiny, and God used a man named Simon to help carry Jesus' cross. God is your refuge; run to Him for help first, before anyone or anything else, but don't recoil from those around you who offer their assistance, because God will often use people to bring the help you need.

When we need help and we aren't receiving it, it's very easy to feel alone in our struggle. We think that no one cares or understands what we are going through. But this is a lie, and the truth is others do care, and many have been through what you are experiencing in your life. God can use these people to encourage and strengthen you.

That being said, whether friends come to your rescue or not, God will move heaven and earth if need be to help you. His Word is the surest foundation in this world, and when you trust in it, the answer will come.

It is in His Word that God tells us to bear one another's burdens, to pray for each other, and to be sensitive to the needs of others. We can get so focused on our own problems that we no longer see the hurts and challenges of those around us. It's through helping others that we ourselves find help. When you are scared, stressed, worried, and tired, choose to surrender your circumstances over to God so you can help someone else. That act of faith will create distance between you and your problems. By focusing on others instead of obsessing about your own problems, you will find you regain the ability to smile in the midst of the mess. Cast the whole of your burden on the Lord, and choose to help others while He in turn helps you.

Prayer

Lord, in Your Word, You say to come to You when I am in need, and that I will find help. I am asking You now to help me. Lord, thank You for Your love and faithfulness. Thank You for comfort and peace, wisdom and guidance. It blesses me to call You "Father." You know exactly what I'm going through and exactly what I need. I cast all of my worries, all of my fears, and all of my anxiety on You, Lord. Help me not to be so focused on my own needs that I forget to reach out and help those around me. Help me to encourage and comfort others. Let Your love, life, and light shine through me to the world around me. Amen.

Scriptures

For we do not have a High Priest Who is unable to understand and sympathize and have a shared feeling with our weaknesses and infirmities and liability to the assaults of temptation, but One Who has been tempted in every respect as we are, yet without sinning. Let us then fearlessly and confidently and boldly draw near to the throne of grace (the throne of God's unmerited favor to us sinners), that we may receive mercy for our failures and find grace to help in good time for every need appropriate help and well-timed help, coming just when we need it.

—Hebrews 4:15-16 AMPC

"The one who blesses others is abundantly blessed; those who help others are helped."

—Proverbs 11:25 MSG

"You're blessed when you care. At the moment of being 'care-full,' you find yourselves cared for."

—Matthew 5:7 MSG

God is our refuge and strength, a very present help in trouble.

—Psalm 46:1 KJV

"No one is useless in this world who lightens the burdens of another."

—CHARLES DICKENS

"Never give in, never give in, never, never, never, in nothing great or small, large or petty, never give in except to convictions of honor and good sense. Never yield to force; never yield to the apparently overwhelming might of the enemy."

—WINSTON CHURCHILL

KNOCKED DOWN, BUT NOT OUT

It's not how hard you fall when you are hit that shows your merit, it's how hard you hit back. The greatest men and women have been knocked off their feet due to a crisis at hand, but they didn't stay there. Even Jesus buckled under the weight of the cross, but He got back up.

Life can deal some pretty hard blows. We can get, as the proverbial phrase goes, our feet knocked out from under us. This is to be expected and not feared. Regardless of your station or your situation in life, crisis is inevitable. Loss, sickness, betrayal, and failures can leave you feeling hopeless in the wake of wasted time and shattered dreams.

But be encouraged, though hard times come, with God they cannot last. The Apostle Paul put it this way in 2 Corinthians 4:8-9 (NIRV) "We are pushed hard from all sides. But we are not beaten down. We are bewildered. But that doesn't make us lose hope. Others make us suffer. But God does not desert us. **We are knocked down. But we are not knocked out.**"

Don't let sickness and disease take your joy, don't let the pain of your current situation blind you to the hope of your future in Christ. You are not defeated when you get knocked down, only when you stay down. As you trust in the Lord, He will cause you to rise from the depths of discouragement and despair to a place of victory.

Dare to try again, to dream again, to overcome that which seems insurmountable. Even if you feel afraid, insecure, and weak, press on. All God needs is a step of faith and He'll meet you right where you are. His strength, His courage, and His confidence will be instilled within you with every step you take. Be audacious enough to take a step of faith, knowing that God will make a way.

Prayer

Lord, thank You for being my refuge, I know when I am hardest hit I can find comfort in Your presence. I can't do it alone, but I know I am not alone. Thank You for loving me, caring for me, for keeping Your promises.

I ask for Your strength to get back up when my own strength has failed. I know that You are my source of strength, hope, and joy. Help me to turn to You and Your Word first for help, instead of as a last resort. Remind me who I am in the midst of failures, so that I may rise again and proclaim Your goodness. Fill me with Your joy and peace. Help me to plug into Your resurrection power that You have made available to all believers. Thank You for courage, strength, and the fortitude to rise up and press on. Amen.

Scriptures

We are hedged in (pressed) on every side troubled and oppressed in every way, but not cramped or crushed; we suffer embarrassments and are perplexed and unable to find a way out, but not driven to despair; We are pursued (persecuted and hard driven), but not deserted to stand alone; we are struck down to the ground, but never struck out and destroyed.

—2 Corinthians 4:8-9 AMPC

The godly may trip seven times, but they will get up again. But one disaster is enough to overthrow the wicked.

—Proverbs 24:16 NLT

The Lord helps the fallen and lifts those bent beneath their loads.

—Psalm 145:14 NLT

Is anyone crying for help? God is listening, ready to rescue you. If your heart is broken, you'll find God right there; If you're kicked in the gut, He'll help you catch your breath. Disciples so often get into trouble; still, God is there every time.

—Psalm 34:17-19 MSG

"Count your blessings. Once you realize how valuable you are and how much you have going for you, the smiles will return, the sun will break out, the music will play, and you will finally be able to move forward with the life that God intended for you with grace, strength, courage, and confidence."

—Og Mandino

Loss

One thing that is universal to the human experience is loss. It's a sobering truth that while we are on this earth there is a beginning and an end to everything. Loss strikes in many different ways—a job, a relationship, the life of a loved one, your influence, your purpose, or simply your ability to do what you once could. Knowing that loss is an inevitable event we all must experience, it's so critical that we learn how to navigate all the pain, confusion, and frustration that occurs when we lose something or someone. Dealing with loss is a process, and it's OK to have feelings of grief, hurt, and confusion, but when you dwell on the pain of loss for too long it can monopolize your life and hinder your ability to heal.

When we experience loss, an emptiness is created that is proportional to how significant the thing was to us that we lost. Too often we try to fill the emptiness with the wrong stuff. We'll fill it up with distractions, thinking that the pain will go away if we don't think about it, but we end up only making our suffering longer. We may try to medicate our emptiness with drugs or alcohol, but we end up making the hole in our lives bigger by the self-destructive nature of substance abuse.

We could try to fill the emptiness with revenge and hatred, blaming others for its existence in the first place. The problem with these methods of dealing with loss is that we are running away from our hurt instead of running to God with our hurt. As you hope in God, you don't have to know how you will make it through, just know that you will—that sometime, somehow, everything will be OK because God is with you.

As you lean on God, the emptiness will begin to fade as God's life, love, and light takes its place.

Prayer

Lord, I know You know what loss is like. You lost Your most beloved Son, for the sake of gaining me. Strengthen me, Lord. Encourage me, teach me how to look to You when my emotions are running wild, and my heart heavy. I know You love me, I know You are a good God, but Lord, if I'm being honest, what I feel and what I know aren't lining up right now. Lord, I ask You to heal my heart, fill the gaps of my life left by loss with the hope that is found in You. You are more than enough for every need and every void that I have. Thank You, Lord, for Your help. Amen.

Scriptures

The Lord is close to the brokenhearted; he rescues those whose spirits are crushed.

—Psalm 34:18 NLT

He heals the brokenhearted and binds up their wounds curing their pains and their sorrows.

—Psalm 147:3 AMPC

Do not let your hearts be troubled (distressed, agitated). You believe in and adhere to and trust in and rely on God; believe in and adhere to and trust in and rely also on Me.

—John 14:1 AMPC

God will wipe away every tear from their eyes; and death shall be no more, neither shall there be anguish (sorrow and mourning) nor grief nor pain any more, for the old conditions and the former order of things have passed away.

—Revelation 21:4 AMPC

There is a great darkness
that doesn't wait for night,
A cold, empty void that hides the light.
It's the end to every beginning,
Feels as if your enemy is winning.
This cancer of the earth,
inescapable since birth.
We were not made for death,
To feel the pain of love's last breath,
The sin that brought loss to our homes,
Has been forgiven but its child still roams,
With its claws sharp but its sting removed,
The pain cuts deep but its poison subdued,
You have a Daddy above,
The purest light named Love,
Ready to pierce the void,
So you won't be destroyed
Lean on Him and the pain will slowly fade,
As the darkness turns to shade,
And the hope of tomorrow,
Begins to lessen yesterday's sorrow.

—JAKE PROVANCE

"I've missed more than 9000 shots in my career. I've lost almost 300 games. 26 times, I've been trusted to take the game winning shot and missed. I've failed over and over and over again in my life. And that is why I succeed."

—Michael Jordan

DON'T QUIT

We all feel like giving up and quitting at one point or another, but don't give in to despair. God has a plan for you, and your breakthrough is right around the corner if you will only press on.

When you've spent year after year weathering your storm, but you have reached the limit of your endurance, *Don't Quit.* When you've been sick so long in your body that you become sick in your soul, *Don't Quit.* When depression, fear, and worry have stressed you to the point of despair, *Don't Quit.* When your circumstances are dire and they seem endless, *Don't Quit.* You don't have to know how you will make it through, just know with God, you *will* make it through if you *Don't Quit.*

The midnight hour comes to everyone—we are not immune because we are Christians.

The Bible puts it like this, "the rain falls on the just, and the unjust." So do not fear or fret when faced with dire circumstances. God knew you would be presented with challenges, that's why He gave us His Word to see you through life's difficulties.

God is with you. God is for you. God is on your side! The same Spirit that raised Christ from the dead resides in you! Activate it by reading God's Word, speaking the truth found in it over your life, and acting upon it. By doing so, it will revitalize your body, fill your mind with peace, permeate your heart with joy, and flood your resolve with strength to face any trial and weather any storm.

So regardless of how dark it may look or feel, let the power, comfort, and light of the Word of God steady your heart and guide you out of your current difficulties. It's the time to stand up and fight back, to face your challenges with an indomitable spirit of an overcomer. Though the night may seem unending and inescapable, the light of dawn is inevitable if you *Don't Quit*!

Prayer

Thank You, Lord, that I am alive. You have kept me safe, You have delivered me from terrible situations. You have made a way for me when there was no way. Thank You, God. Father, I ask that You would remind me of all the times You've delivered me when I'm tempted to doubt. When I'm hardest hit, help me to stay united with You. I ask for peace, clarity of mind, strength, and joy to make it through, and hope for the future. You have been, are, and always will be, by my side; remind me of that and help me take comfort in Your words. Help me to fight through discouragement, disappointment, and setbacks. I know that I'm destined to win if I won't quit. Amen.

Scriptures

"I have told you these things, so that in Me you may have perfect peace and confidence. In the world you have tribulation and trials and distress and frustration; but be of good cheer take courage; be confident, certain, undaunted! For I have overcome the world. I have deprived it of power to harm you and have conquered it for you."

—John 16:33 AMPC

Now thanks be unto God, which always causeth us to triumph in Christ, and maketh manifest the savour of his knowledge by us in every place.

—2 Corinthians 2:14 KJV

But thanks be to God, Who gives us the victory making us conquerors through our Lord Jesus Christ.

—1 Corinthians 15:57 AMPC

DON'T QUIT
by John Greenleaf Whittier

When things go wrong as they sometimes will,
When the road you're trudging seems all up hill,
When the funds are low and the debts are high
And you want to smile, but you have to sigh,
When care is pressing you down a bit,
Rest if you must, but don't you quit.
Life is strange with its twists and turns
As every one of us sometimes learns
And many a failure comes about
When he might have won had he stuck it out;
Don't give up though the pace seems slow –
You may succeed with another blow.
Success is failure turned inside out—
The silver tint of the clouds of doubt,
And you never can tell just how close you are,
It may be near when it seems so far;
So stick to the fight when you're hardest hit—
It's when things seem worst that you must not quit.

"If there was ever a secret for unleashing God's powerful peace in a situation, it's developing a heart of true thanksgiving."

—LYSA TERKEURST

THANKFULNESS

When our circumstances have beaten us up, our flesh can speak so loudly that we can't hear the voice of hope, the voice of God. It's all too easy to focus on the negativity of life and our current situation; to fill our minds with negative thoughts and our mouths with doubts and complaints. This will drain us of our strength, joy, and peace. It's because of times like these that the Bible says "when" you are faced with a spirit of heaviness, to "put on" a garment of praise.

When God said "when" and not "if," it's Him recognizing and warning us that we all will face a spirit of heaviness and have opportunities to be depressed, worried, and fearful. But "put on" is God encouraging us that we don't have to stay there—we can make a conscious choice to clothe ourselves with thankfulness.

In the toughest moments in your life, you might think,

Well, what do I have to be thankful for?

And if you were only looking at your situation, that might be a reasonable question. But don't let the current problem or situation you are in blind you to all that God has done for you, and in you. If nothing else, you get to spend eternity with God. That ought to be enough to be excited about for the rest of your life!

When we are thankful, it helps keep our focus on God and brings a perspective of hope. Seeing our life, with all its ups and downs, through the eyes of hope will bring us peace and security, as we rest in the truth that with God as our Father, everything is going to work out. There is no greater expression of your faith then to lift your voice and thank God for all He's done, is doing, and will do, right there in the midst of the storm.

Prayer

There's nothing better than to practice thankfulness in prayer. God's Word says that every good thing comes from Him. So take a few moments and thank God for everything good in your life.

Scriptures

Rejoice always, pray continually, give thanks in all circumstances, for this is God's will for you in Christ Jesus.

—1 Thessalonians 5:16-18 NIV

And whatever you do, whether in word or deed, do it all in the name of the Lord Jesus, giving thanks to God the Father through him.

—Colossians 3:17 NIV

Be earnest and unwearied and steadfast in your prayer life, being both alert and intent in your praying with thanksgiving.

—Colossians 4:2 AMPC

Be careful for nothing; but in everything by prayer and supplication with thanksgiving let your requests be made known unto God.

—Philippians 4:6 KJV

Thank goodness for all of the things you are not!
Thank goodness you're not
something someone forgot,
and left all alone in some punkerish place
like a rusty tin coat hanger hanging in space.
That's why I say "Duckie!
don't grumble! don't stew!
some critters are much-much,
oh, ever so much-much,
so muchly much-much more unlucky than you!"

—Dr. Seuss

"Your time is limited, so don't waste it living someone else's life. Don't be trapped by dogma—which is living with the results of other people's thinking. Don't let the noise of others' opinions drown out your own inner voice. And most important, have the courage to follow your heart and intuition."

—STEVE JOBS

TRAPPED

If you have exhausted all your options and giving up seems to be the only choice that you have left; if things feel as if they will never change, and you feel helpless and hopeless at the same time; if you feel like you've lost control over your life, and you question if it is even worth living—if you have felt these things, then you know what it is like to feel trapped. It is an unfortunate truth that many will find themselves feeling helpless, hopeless, and alone in a room with no doors.

The only way to escape, the only way out, is to let God in.

Where the spirit of the Lord is, there is freedom. God is the God of hope, and the moment you let him into your situation, you let hope in. In His presence there is fullness of joy, because the darkness of fear and deception cannot exist in the light of God's perfect love for you. To believe you are trapped is to believe a lie. You are never truly trapped if you are a Christian. God can, and will make a way out for you if you will trust in Him, and keep on trusting in Him.

When there seems to be no way, God will make a way. Don't give into the temptation to give up your faith, your joy, and your hope. Hear it from His own words found in 1 Corinthians 10:13 AMP: "No temptation regardless of its source has overtaken *or* enticed you that is not common to human experience nor is any temptation unusual or beyond human resistance; but God is faithful to His word—He is compassionate and trustworthy, and He will not let you be tempted beyond your ability to resist, but along with the temptation He has in the past and is now and will always provide the way out as well, so that you will be able to endure it without yielding, and will overcome temptation with joy."

<u>Prayer</u>

Lord I know that according to Your Word, wherever You are, there is freedom. I know that You will never leave me nor forsake me, but the feelings of being trapped coming from everything I see can overwhelm me. So by faith, I cast the weight of my responsibilities off my shoulders and onto yours. I place my pain, my confusion, and my hopelessness at Your feet and I ask for Your peace and joy to take their place. I ask for wisdom and guidance for my next step. Help me to hope again, to live boldly and confidently in remembrance of your promises towards me, and to be assured beyond any doubt that you will make a way for me. Thank you, Lord. Amen.

Scriptures

"If you'll hold on to me for dear life," says God, "I'll get you out of any trouble. I'll give you the best of care if you'll only get to know and trust me. Call me and I'll answer, be at your side in bad times; I'll rescue you, then throw you a party. I'll give you a long life, give you a long drink of salvation!"

—Psalm 91:14-16 MSG

For the Lord is the Spirit, and wherever the Spirit of the Lord is, there is freedom.

—2 Corinthians 3:17 NLT

"But I'll take the hand of those who don't know the way, who can't see where they're going. I'll be a personal guide to them, directing them through unknown country. I'll be right there to show them what roads to take, make sure they don't fall into the ditch. These are the things I'll be doing for them—sticking with them, not leaving them for a minute."

—Isaiah 42:16 MSG

"Twenty years from now you will be more disappointed by the things that you didn't do than by the ones you did do. So throw off the bowlines. Sail away from the safe harbor. Catch the trade winds in your sails. Explore. Dream. Discover."

—Mark Twain

"In the same way the sun never grows weary of shining, nor a stream of flowing, it is God's nature to keep His promises. Therefore, go immediately to His throne and say, 'Do as You promised.'"

—CHARLES SPURGEON

WEARINESS

Weariness is not being tired at the end of the day, nor a lack of energy when starting the day. Weariness is when you become tired in your soul; the kind of tired you can't sleep off; when your situation feels endless; and your perspective is tainted with hopelessness. Weariness can creep into your life in many different ways. You can become weary from the grind of everyday life, from trying to balance all your responsibilities, from doing the right thing without recognition or reward, from years of unfulfilled potential and dreams, from overcommitting yourself, or from trying to keep up daily appearances.

It's easy to settle for the fake peace the world prescribes, using entertainment, medications, and alcohol to escape the barrage of pressures and responsibilities that assail our lives daily. The problem with this kind of momentary cease fire is we have to come back to the same life we tried to forget. Whatever the cause for the weariness in your life, the answer is the same. Jesus said, "come to me all who are weary and I will give you rest."

God never meant for us to be dependent on anyone or anything besides Himself. The same peace that Jesus operated in is available for us, to live in a tranquil state, with our soul secured due to our trust in God. If you are not resting on the inside, with a mind quieted by this peace, then you cannot rest on the outside, finding rejuvenation for your body. So carve out time every day to spend with God to enjoy and refresh yourself in His Word. Seek out wisdom for what commitments you need to maintain and which ones you need to let go. Finally, rest in the Lord, casting all the weight of your life and its problems on Him, because you know He'll take care of you.

Life can be a dull struggle for survival, barely staying afloat in the sea of endless responsibilities and expectations, or life can be a glorious adventure that you undertake with your friends, family, and your God.

<u>Prayer</u>

Lord, thank You that I am never alone, that You are always with me, and that when I'm exhausted I know that I can lean on You and You'll be there for me. I ask for renewed strength and a renewed sense of purpose. Guide me with Your Word and Your peace. Create space in my days where I can catch my breath with You, where I can truly rest in Your arms. Help me keep my focus on You, instead of the trials I go through. Encourage and comfort me, when the grind of life saps my energy. Thank You, Lord. Amen.

Scriptures

And let us not grow weary while doing good, for in due season we shall reap if we do not lose heart.

—Galatians 6:9 NKJV

Truly my soul finds rest in God; my salvation comes from him.

—Psalm 62:1 NIV

In peace I will lie down and sleep, for you alone, O Lord, will keep me safe.

—Psalm 4:8 NLT

But those who wait for the Lord who expect, look for, and hope in Him shall change and renew their strength and power; they shall lift their wings and mount up close to God as eagles mount up to the sun; they shall run and not be weary, they shall walk and not faint or become tired.

—Isaiah 40:31 AMPC

"Are you tired? Worn out? Burned out on religion? Come to me. Get away with me and you'll recover your life. I'll show you how to take a real rest. Walk with me and work with me—watch how I do it. Learn the unforced rhythms of grace. I won't lay anything heavy or ill-fitting on you. Keep company with me and you'll learn to live freely and lightly."

—Jesus (Matthew 11:28-30 MSG)

"The Christian life is not a constant high. I have my moments of deep discouragement. I have to go to God in prayer with tears in my eyes, and say, 'O God, forgive me,' or 'Help me.'"

—BILLY GRAHAM

DISCOURAGEMENT

Discouragement can sneak up on us. Especially if we have been dealing with some adverse circumstances for an extended period of time. It's more than just being disappointed, discontented, or frustrated. It's much deeper, and much more sinister. It is a negative spiritual force that can rob you of your joy and peace. It can produce a sense of hopelessness that can paralyze your life and cloud your perspective.

Discouragement drains us of our strength and confidence, reminds us of our failures, and causes us to forget our blessings. It is the gateway through which many life-altering struggles are formed, like depression and insecurity. It's a subtle pain that darkens the brightest of moments.

We all face the reality that we in and of ourselves are not good enough, smart enough, or talented enough to accomplish what we are truly meant for. That's because we need God in us to achieve our destiny. The problem is when you derive your identity, your happiness, and your strength through what you have or haven't done, you are setting yourself up to be discouraged and hurt.

God is our source of happiness, He is our source of strength, and He is what we base our self-worth on, not other people or circumstances. So spend time reading His words and thinking on His promises. Focus on Him and all the blessings in your life instead of all the problems. Let God love you—through praise, through worship, through prayer, and through His Word. To be discouraged is to believe a lie, for when you truly believe what God's Word says about you, your heart will be filled with confident joy.

<u>Prayer</u>

Lord, You are the God who encourages. Your joy is my strength, Your peace is my guide, and Your presence is my protection. I know that though my strength may fail, Your strength will pick up the slack. I know that even when I feel hurt and alone, You are with me ready to help me. So I ask for that very thing. Remind me You are near to me, remind me I'm Yours, and that Your plans for me are greater than any closed door, any heartbreaking situation, and any setback. With You by my side as my encourager, I know that I will be OK. Thank You, Lord. Amen.

Scriptures

Don't be afraid, for I am with you. Don't be discouraged, for I am your God. I will strengthen you and help you. I will hold you up with my victorious right hand.

—Isaiah 41:10 NLT

"This is my command—be strong and courageous! Do not be afraid or discouraged. For the Lord your God is with you wherever you go."

—Joshua 1:9 NLT

But God, who encourages those who are discouraged, encouraged us by the arrival of Titus.

—2 Corinthians 7:6 NLT

Therefore we do not become discouraged (utterly spiritless, exhausted, and wearied out through fear). Though our outer man is progressively decaying and wasting away, yet our inner self is being progressively renewed day after day.

—2 Corinthians 4:16 AMPC

"Resist discouragement by speaking His Word over your future. Keep standing. Keep hoping; keep believing because He is working behind the scenes. He's going to accelerate your times and lead you into the life of victory He has for you."

—JOEL OSTEEN

"Never look back unless you are planning to go that way."

—Henry David Thoreau

THE PAST

We have all lived through things or done things in our past that we are not proud of. It may be a small nagging memory that pops up now and then that leaves a sour taste in your mouth, or it can be a haunting regret that plagues your thought life with shame nearly every day. This is no way to live, and God never intended for you to bear such weight. The good news is, you don't have to any longer. Regardless of the mistakes you've made, or even crimes like abuse that have been committed against you, there is healing and freedom available to you. You can learn from your past, but don't dwell there. You can't go forward looking backward. If you're not careful, you can miss the joy of today and the victories of tomorrow by focusing on the failures of the past. You must replace your thoughts of regret and shame by renewing your mind with the Word of God. Instead of remembering all the hurts and pains of the past, remember all the things that God has done for you. Remember that God bought you back from sin, shame, and destruction. Remember that He adopted you into His family. Remember that He made you blameless, pure, and holy. Remember that He has forgiven and forgotten every mistake you've made!

God doesn't see you in the light of your past, He sees you in the light of His Son's sacrifice! You are righteous, in right standing with your Father, God. When He looks at you He sees His beautiful creation, His best friend, His child.

You have the love of God to heal your heart from the pain of your past; to place a new identity upon you and a new power within you. Your present situation is changeable, and the future of your dreams attainable! With His love healing your past, His strength reinforcing your present, and the power of His promises guaranteeing your future, you are defined by and destined for greatness.

<u>Prayer</u>

Thank You, Lord, for Your forgiveness, for Your grace, and for Your mercy. You said in Your Word that You have forgiven and forgotten my sins. Help me to forgive myself and let go of my past. Lord, I know my future is much too important. I know You have a plan and purpose for me. I ask for Your help to govern my perspective according to Your Word and not according to my experiences. Help me to not build upon my experience but build upon Your Word. Help me to lean on You, instead of my own understanding. Help me to move on with my life, to leave the past behind me, and reach toward the future you have planned for me. Amen.

Scriptures

"Forget the former things; do not dwell on the past. See, I am doing a new thing! Now it springs up; do you not perceive it? I am making a way in the wilderness and streams in the wasteland."

—Isaiah 43:18-19 NIV

Therefore if any man be in Christ, he is a new creature: old things are passed away; behold, all things are become new.

—2 Corinthians 5:17 KJV

No, dear brothers and sisters, I have not achieved it, but I focus on this one thing: forgetting the past and looking forward to what lies ahead, I press on to reach the end of the race and receive the heavenly prize for which God, through Christ Jesus, is calling us.

—Philippians 3:13-14 NLT

"Renew, release, let go. Yesterday's gone. There's nothing you can do to bring it back. You can't should've done something. You can only DO something. Renew yourself. Release that attachment. Today is a new day!"

—STEVE MARABOLI

"Choices are the hinges of destiny."

—EDWIN MARKHAM

It's a Choice

Letting your heart not be troubled is a choice. A choice to cast all of your worries, all of your anxiety, and all of your fears onto your Heavenly Father. A choice to seek help for others when they need help. A choice to find good in any situation. A choice to smile without a reason and to love without a cause. A choice to hope in hopeless situations. A choice to trust God in the midst of a treacherous storm, and to rejoice with Him in the midst of the best life has to offer.

A choice to surrender control of your life over to your Heavenly Father. A choice to let God in so He can then get you out. A choice to believe your Father's Word over the world's lies. A choice to remember your blessings instead of your mistakes. A choice to lean on God for strength when you feel you can't take another step. A choice to fill the gaps of your abilities with faith in God's. A choice to fill the hole created by loss with God's love. A choice to be lost in God's presence instead of an addiction. A choice to give up walking alone and accept the helping hand of your Father. A choice to fight against what is evil, and to love what is good.

A choice to believe in God when no one on this earth believes in you, because He believes in you. A choice to think on what is good and not perversion. A choice of a joyful attitude, and a cheerful disposition.

The truth is God is your daddy, and the greatest gift that He has given you is the ability to choose Him. For it can be your choice, in the midst of the mess this world is in, with billions of options for you to choose over Him, to still surrender all that you are, and run into His loving arms and say "I choose you." Choose Him . . . choose to let your heart not be troubled.

Prayer

Lord, I understand that my choices have an impact on my life. I ask for guidance and direction for the choices that I make. Help me to discern Your will, and to hear Your voice. I ask for wisdom in all my affairs. Help me not to be influenced in my decision making by my emotions, nor by the opinions of others. Help me to slow down, and relax when I feel pressured, that I would make the right choice. Amen.

Scriptures

"Today I have given you the choice between life and death, between blessings and curses. Now I call on heaven and earth to witness the choice you make. Oh, that you would choose life, so that you and your descendants might live!"

—Deuteronomy 30:19 NLT

My counsel is this: Live freely, animated and motivated by God's Spirit. Then you won't feed the compulsions of selfishness. For there is a root of sinful self-interest in us that is at odds with a free spirit, just as the free spirit is incompatible with selfishness. These two ways of life are antithetical, so that you cannot live at times one way and at times another way according to how you feel on any given day. Why don't you choose to be led by the Spirit and so escape the erratic compulsions of a law-dominated existence?

—Galatians 5:16-18 (MSG)

"Everything can be taken from a man but one thing: the last of human freedoms—to choose one's attitude in any given set of circumstances, to choose one's own way."

—Viktor E. Frankl
(Holocaust survivor)

Other inspirational books by Jake & Keith Provance

Keep Calm and Trust God -Volume 1

Keep Calm and Trust God – Volume 2

I AM What the Bible Says I AM

Scriptural Prayers for Victorious Living

Keep Calm and Trust God (Gift Edition)

Coming Soon

I Have What the Bible Says I Have

I Can Do What the Bible Says I Can